SIGNAL BOXES AND SEMAPHORES

The Decline

GORDON D. WEBSTER

AMBERLEY

All photographs were taken by the author unless otherwise noted.

Front Cover: Class 66 No. 66078 passes the now-closed Barnetby East signal box, Humberside, with a coal train from Immingham.

Back Cover: Blair Atholl station, Perthshire, on the Highland main line.

First published 2016

Amberley Publishing
The Hill, Stroud,
Gloucestershire, GL5 4EP

www.amberley-books.com

ISBN: 978 1 4456 5617 5 (print)
ISBN: 978 1 4456 5618 2 (ebook)

British Library Cataloguing in Publication Data.
A catalogue record for this book is available from the British Library.

Typeset in 10pt on 13pt Celeste.
Typesetting by Amberley Publishing.
Printed in the UK.

Index

Abbotsbury, Abbotsbury Abbey, 17, 23, 24, 25, 42
Anglican Friars, 98
Beaminster, 2, 3, 4, 5, 11, 15, 19, 29, 31, 35, 43, 44, 49, 51, 53, 54, 60, 62, 63, 65, 66, 67, 68, 69, 70, 72, 77, 89, 91, 92, 95, 96, 100, 103, 104, 105, 133
blacksmith, 81, 87, 91, 103
boar, 19, 109
Boer War, 58, 65, 133
Catholic, see Roman Catholic
Celtic fields, 10
chalk pits, 61, 63
chantry chapel, 22, 23, 31, 38
Cifrewast, Cyfrewast, Sifrewast, 11, 12, 14, 16, 17, 18, 20, 127
Civil War, 28, 29, 42, 43, 46
Common Lane, 15, 19
Count Mortain, 9
crenellated, 12
deer park, 13, 18, 19, 20, 26, 36, 43, 44, 48, 56, 95
dewponds, 75
Domesday, 8, 9, 10, 16, 19, 27
Dorset labourer, 73
Dorset Ridgeway, 3, 7, 9, 15
dovecote, 12, 13
Duke of Bolton, 28, 46, 47, 50, 121, 127
Duke of Cleveland 46, 58, 64
Earl of Sandwich, 35, 50, 59, 60, 64, 65, 69, 71, 78, 102, 127
Eggardon, 3, 5, 8, 9, 11, 16, 17, 19, 24, 43, 48, 50, 70
Electricity, 104
factory, 60, 66
First World War, 87, 94, 96, 97
flood, 93, 106
fulling mill, 14, 51, 52
Great Ridgeway, 3, 5, 7
Green Lane, 9, 14, 15, 19, 49, 54, 56, 59, 61, 72, 75, 100
grist mill, 14, 52
Hardy, Thomas 3, 63, 89
hayward, 52, 55
Higher Kingcombe, 1, 15, 63, 66
Hine, 51, 53, 62, 77
Home Guard, 82, 95

Hooke Court, 1, 3, 4, 5, 6, 8, 11, 12, 13, 14, 15, 16, 17, 19, 21, 22, 23, 25, 28, 31, 32, 33, 36, 42, 43, 47, 48, 49, 50, 56, 58, 59, 60, 61, 64, 65, 69, 78, 82, 83, 84, 87, 89, 90, 92, 98, 100, 101, 102, 104, 105, 108, 132, 133
Hooke Farm, 54, 64, 71, 74, 91, 108
Hooke Park, 2, 15, 24, 36, 39, 43, 44, 48, 50, 56, 89, 94, 97, 105, 109
John Munden, 36
Juniper House, 61, 69, 84, 91, 97, 100, 101
Justices of the Peace, 21
Knights-in-the-Bottom, Knights Bottom, 3, 4, 9, 15, 50, 55, 56, 59, 90, 100, 104
lime kiln, 57
Lower Kingcombe, 5, 15, 66, 69
magistrates, 21, 27, 33, 42, 47, 51
Maiden Newton, 1, 6, 15, 29, 43, 69, 71, 72, 92, 94, 100, 101, 105
Manor Farm, 15, 61, 64, 72, 73, 90, 92, 107
Manorial Court, 4, 21, 51, 52, 53, 54, 67, 69, 124, 124, 127
Marquis of Winchester, 25, 28, 32, 33, 35, 36, 42, 43, 45, 50
Masons Arms, 50, 55, 59, 70, 131
Mautravers, 17, 21, 23
Mill Lane, 15
miller, 17, 18, 52, 53, 54, 60, 68, 70, 122
Minterne, Mintern, 33, 36, 50, 52, 54, 55, 65, 86, 122, 123, 124, 125, 126, 131
moat, 11
Montagu, 35, 50
Mount Pleasant, 1, 5
Mundens of Coltleigh, 36
Neolithic, 10
Normans, 19
Old School House, 89, 100, 104
Parish Meeting, 4, 59, 103, 106
Park Pond, 8, 13, 15, 20, 43, 47, 63, 84
Parochial Church Council, 93, 103
Parsonage Coppice, 49, 95, 109
Paulet, 25, 29, 32, 33, 35, 36, 46, 50
Paulet Arms, 81, 89, 91, 104, 108, 131
Pipsford Farm, 54
police, Police Station, 68, 130
Pope family, 51, 53, 54, 74, 125
post office, 60, 75, 89, 91, 93
postman, 91

Powerstock, 2, 4, 11, 14, 18, 23, 26, 29, 33, 50, 93

Powerstock Common, 19

Prince of Wales, 69, 78

Puritan, 29, 31, 32, 36, 41, 42, 128

Rampisham Hill, 14, 15, 49, 55, 87

Rampisham Radio Masts, 105

rector, 14, 18, 32, 36, 51, 60, 64, 71, 87, 90, 92, 95, 102, 128

rectory, 60, 64, 87, 91, 104, 105

River Hooke, 1

Robert Willoughby, Lord Brooke, 25, 32, 128

Roman, 3, 5, 6, 8, 9, 10, 13, 56

Roman Catholic, 28, 29, 31, 32, 35, 36, 41, 46

St. Francis School for Boys, 83, 102, 105, 110

Salt family, 87, 89, 90, 92, 93, 94, 106

Saxon, 5, 6, 13, 17

Second World War, 21, 57, 59, 87, 89, 91, 95, 96, 97, 102, 108, 109

Sherborne Abbey, 16, 24,

Sifrewast. See Cyfrewast.

smugglers, 50, 55

St. Giles, 4, 14, 22, 26, 31, 37, 40, 49, 59, 61, 62, 63, 102, 103, 127

Stafford, Humphry, 17, 21, 22, 23, 24, 25, 26, 31, 32, 128

Stapleford, 3, 9, 13, 14, 16, 18, 21, 22, 23, 27, 45, 47, 128

Sunday School, 69, 91, 92

telephone kiosk, 81, 89, 91

tithingman, 19, 21, 52, 55, 65, 122

Toller Down, 3, 10, 15, 26, 27, 45, 48, 57, 63, 105

Toller Porcorum, 14, 15, 18, 24, 26, 29, 33, 45, 49, 64, 69, 75, 87, 89, 97, 102, 104, 106, 109

Toller Whelme, 1, 15, 25, 35, 36, 43, 51, 54, 63, 69, 74, 127, 128

tucking mill, see fulling mill

village school, 80, 89

Warren Hill, 1, 3, 5, 9, 19, 48, 50, 56, 65, 69, 75, 101

water, 3, 4, 5, 6, 9, 11, 13, 14, 15, 19, 26, 38, 41, 57, 60, 66, 71, 73, 75, 79, 90, 91, 94, 96, 105, 106

Watercress, 75, 84, 96, 97, 107

Westcombe coppice, 33, 43, 44, 57, 63, 74, 109

Women's Institute, W.I., 93

Women's Land Army, 96

workhouse, 67

Contents

Acknowledgements 4

Introduction 5

Chapter 1 North West 9

Chapter 2 North East 22

Chapter 3 Scotland 38

Chapter 4 Wales and Borders 56

Chapter 5 South West 69

Chapter 6 Anglia and South East 78

Chapter 7 Heritage Signal Boxes 87

Bibliography 96

Acknowledgements

Huge thanks to the staff at Network Rail, included below, who assisted with research and photographs, particularly the signallers and Local Operations Managers who allowed access to their boxes. To friends and family for their support, especially my father David Webster. He is one of the few who had the foresight to photograph loco-hauled trains and semaphores while they still co-existed on some of the less well-known scenic lines. To my Friends of the West Highland Lines colleague Nick Jones who has been particularly helpful with his vast store of knowledge and photographs. To Alex Campbell, Nick Garnham, Jeremy Jackson, Phil Lucas, Andy Savage, Andy Scobie, Stuart Scott, John Shinie, Paul Stewart and the Branch Line Society, James Wilkin and John Yellowlees.

Of course, the project would not have been possible without the support of Georgina Coleby, Connor Stait and everyone at Amberley Publishing. I also want to acknowledge the superb work of the Railway Heritage Trust, Signalling Record Society and Film Archive of Railway Signalling and People (FARSAP) signalling archive.

Introduction

The 1960s was a defining decade for Britain's railways, with the end of steam, the Beeching cuts and with it a huge swathe of line closures. Changes were also afoot in the way trains were signalled, with the advent of British Rail's (BR) Power Signal Boxes (PSBs) or 'Signalling Centres' to control key sections along what were regarded as the principal routes. These 'control room'-type buildings took over from many mechanical signal boxes that had hitherto been in command of train movements ever since the Victorian era. Having a traditional, smaller 'box' with a signalman employed at virtually every station on the network was a dated practice and an expensive burden. Many were at busy urban locations, with the lever frames wired to rows of semaphore signals and mechanical points. In their place came the 'power boxes' and their electrical panels, controlling multiple-aspect colour light signals across much larger square mile sections. Despite this, large concentrations of manual signalling remained and by the 1970s, the lineside infrastructure still looked very much 'steam era'.

Fast-forwarding several decades to the privatised railway world of today, control of train passage has become more centralised still and the majority of mechanical signal boxes have now closed. Yet, a few hundred are remarkably still in use, despite being over a hundred years old in many cases, along some secondary main lines and branch lines. A small number have been modernised internally with lever frames replaced by Entrance-Exit (NX) panels, while some of the semaphore signals have been replaced by colour lights, but still operated from the frame. All are still manned and some remain open both day and night. But for how much longer?

Re-signalling has been a very gradual process from the mid-1990s into the millennium and spending has been carefully concentrated on the routes seen as top-priority. Many long-expected renewals seemed to be getting put on the back-burner until 2010, when Network Rail revealed its National Operating Strategy to cover the next few decades. This watershed project will spell the end for mechanical signalling on the main line once and for all, with most remaining boxes and semaphore signals to disappear over the next fifteen years. In their place will be twelve Regional Operating Centres (ROCs), or Rail Operating Centres as they are now being referred to more and more. Eventually, they will control every route across the country, covering an even bigger geographical radius than the PSBs of the 1960s, which will also shut. Such a vital project has been a long time coming, but on a sad note, it will end a familiar way of life on the railway that goes back generations.

These plans prompted me to get the camera out and record the last signal boxes and semaphores before they are gone for good. In these pages, I hope to have shown the very best remaining examples of boxes, with a particular emphasis on variety of signals, trains and general environment. I have mainly concentrated on those still controlling semaphores to try to capture tradition and help convey the character of the typical rural station of the past. That is, the peace and quiet of the countryside, interrupted by the soft rustling of the signal wires beneath the platform as the semaphore arms are raised (or dropped if they are lower quadrant signals) to warn of an approaching train. If it's quiet you might even hear the noise of the block bells sounding from the box. Garsdale, Dalwhinnie, Par, these are a few examples of where this classic atmosphere can still be experienced.

The majority of signal boxes covered in this study use Absolute Block working, always the traditional type of system used across the British network for double-track main lines. It has been the norm since the late nineteenth century, when early railways used the primitive 'time interval' method; meaning a train would be permitted to leave a station after a sufficient amount of time had elapsed following the passing of the train running in front of it, following a railwayman's hand signals. With no communication between the stations, there was no way of determining the whereabouts of each train and staff worked on the assumption that each one would be running to time and separated far enough that collisions would not happen. Naturally, this unsafe practice did not last and at the same time, fixed wooden signals were invented, superseded midway through the 1800s by the first semaphore signals. These were of the lower quadrant variety, which would be standard until the late 1920s when upper quadrants started to take over.

The 1860s saw the first signal boxes start to appear on the network, with interlocked lever frames. Interlocking prevented a signalman from accidentally setting conflicting movements with the points and signals, for example, routing one oncoming train into the path of another. Various frame designs were installed, some by the pre-Grouping railway companies themselves and some the work of signalling contractors. The most notable were the work of contractors McKenzie & Holland, Stevens & Son and Saxby & Farmer. A good number of these early examples survive in use today.

The seeds were sown as far as boxes and signals were concerned, but it was not until the invention of Absolute Block working that some proper uniformity started to develop across the country. The Regulation of Railways Act 1889 ruled that 'block' working and interlocking had to be in place on all passenger routes across Great Britain and Ireland, and it was during this period that signal box construction really accelerated. Absolute Block would go onto dominate. The fundamentals of this system are that the line is divided into individual 'block' sections, with one section between each signal box. Only a single train is allowed into each block section in any one direction at any time. Bell codes are electrically transmitted from the block instruments in one box to the next, to give authority for trains to enter and exit each section. An example would be on the Cumbrian Coast line between the boxes at Wigton, Maryport and Workington. A train can be travelling along the Wigton–Maryport section, following a train heading south that is within the Maryport–Workington section. However, the Maryport signaller can only give the second train clear signals to pass his or her box once their colleague at Workington Main No. 3 box has confirmed the first train has now exited that section.

The spread of colour light signals was accompanied by Track Circuit Block (TCB) working, which has now replaced Absolute Block across most of the network. This uses electrical devices buried beneath the track to record the current whereabouts of each train, which are simultaneously displayed on the panels in most modern signalling centres. The double-track lines examined in this book by and large still use Absolute Block, but as we shall see later, there is a multitude of other regulations in use for single-track lines.

Furthermore, various methods of working now co-exist along the same sections of railway. A journey from Ayr to Stranraer is a prime example of how complex things can get. A southbound train leaves Ayr at present under the watchful eyes of the West of Scotland Signalling Centre, Glasgow, using TCB. After going from double to a single line at Kilkerran it is worked as Tokenless Block to Girvan. Girvan–Dunragit then uses the well-past-its-sell-by-date Electric Train Tablet system, then from Dunragit to Stranraer it is One Train Working with a staff. To complicate things even further, freight trains heading east out of Ayr use a whole different system – No Signaller Key Token working – to Mauchline!

ROCs will not only save on staff salaries and maintenance costs, but they are being built to kick off a move towards in-cab signalling and a special Traffic Management System (TMS), which will allow more trains to be run more frequently, without compromising safety, and thus cater for the continued growth in rail travel. This long-term plan by Network Rail will see the abolition of all lineside signals, with drivers instead being under the command of monitors inside their cab, which give indications of when to increase speed, stop, etc. This is known as the European Train Control System (ETCS) and will be controlled by the twelve ROCs; the signallers there sending trains a 'movement authority' using GSM-R radio equipment. The TMS will use up-to-date live intelligence to spot potential pathing difficulties before they happen and minimise delays even further. Both ETCS and TMS fall under the overall umbrella term of the European Rail Traffic Management System (ERTMS).

So all this will mark the end of the road for the true signal box, on the main line anyway. Happily, a good number of classic boxes have been preserved thanks to groups such as the Railway Heritage Trust. Those still in operational use are generally very well-kept by Network Rail, following on from their predecessors Railtrack, who started to heavily refurbish most remaining examples in the late 1990s after they fell into disrepair. There are still plenty of interesting signals around too, even a few semaphore distants, though the majority of these have been replaced by colour lights. The distants are particularly inaccessible and difficult to photograph.

Completing this pictorial record has been an enjoyable project and as far as possible, I have tried to make it a historical snapshot of signal boxes and semaphores at the present moment, during their final years. You will notice the High Speed Train (HST), or InterCity 125 as it is often known, has crept in a fair bit, which seemed appropriate given these revolutionary trains reached their fortieth anniversary in 2016. And guess what? After all these years, HSTs still look remarkably modern against a backdrop of semaphore signals!

I am no signalling expert, far from it, and my research has involved very careful analysis of numerical and historical data. Future plans are changing all the time, particular box closure dates, and all information within these pages I believe to be correct at the time of writing. So apologies in advance for any errors that may crop up. Please note that the number of levers given for each box includes any spare levers or spaces where some have been removed from the frame. The interior shots will also hopefully give an idea of a signaller's typical working environment. It is now perhaps more comfortable and aided by computers, but has changed little else over the years.

GDW
Glasgow
August 2016

CHAPTER 1

North West

Some of the most scenic railways in the British Isles lie in north-west England, where the abundance of traditional signalling adds even more to their appeal. The Cumbrian Coast line is the 'long way round' from Carlisle to Lancaster via Barrow-in-Furness, hugging the Irish Sea and Morecambe Bay almost throughout, but the downside is that it is very exposed to storms. A multi-million pound scheme by Network Rail is taking place at the time of writing to protect the most vulnerable sections from erosion and this saw 15,000 tonnes of rock put in place to form a barrier between the beach and track at Parton in spring 2016. The signal box here became so weather-beaten latterly that it had to be held together with metal supports and eventually closed in 2010.

Manual boxes and semaphore signals still dominate along the rest of the Cumbrian Coast, which is mainly double-track, though there are a few short single-line sections, most notably from Whitehaven to Sellafield. All nineteen remaining boxes are to shut down from 2019 to 2021. These are: Wigton, Maryport, Workington Main Nos 2 and 3, Bransty (Whitehaven), St Bees, Sellafield, Drigg, Bootle, Silecroft, Millom, Foxfield, Askam, Park South Junction, Barrow-in-Furness, Dalton Junction, Ulverston, Grange-over-Sands and Arnside. Carnforth Station Junction box will also close.

Four manual gated level crossings – each operated by an individual crossing keeper housed in a portakabin – still survive on the coast. Skelly Crag crossing lies immediately south of Foxfield station, Saltcoats crossing is near Ravenglass, while the other two are situated between Silecroft and Millom. This dated practice continues in many places across England for safety reasons and the crossings should remain manually operated until the rest of the boxes along the line are shut. The portakabins are usually called 'gate boxes', as they are provided solely to control the crossings without regulating block sections, though other gate boxes actually have the appearance of a small signal box.

The most well-known route in the north from a scenic perspective is the Settle & Carlisle (S&C) line, formerly the Midland Railway's (MR) principal express route to Carlisle and Scotland. It has seen many ups and down since the Beeching era, losing most of its traffic and being run down to the point it was almost closed completely in the 1980s. However, a remarkable revival in the 1990s–2000s saw a massive upsurge in freight traffic and increased use by diverted Anglo-Scottish expresses while the West Coast Main Line

(WCML) was being modernised again. The ten manual signal boxes along the route were refurbished to a superb standard in keeping with much of the station buildings but not just cosmetically; all are very much working boxes today, though freight levels have dipped again in recent years.

Some boxes on the S&C, such as Horton-in-Ribblesdale and Dent, would not survive BR's rationalisation, but those at Armathwaite and Settle stations have been restored to magnificent condition by the Friends of the Settle–Carlisle Line. Garsdale was switched out of use for much of the 1980s and 1990s, but was reactivated full time by Railtrack because the line became so busy again. Most S&C boxes share a very recognisable MR design though there are exceptions, for example, Blea Moor is of 1941 London, Midland & Scottish Railway (LMS) vintage and Kirkby Stephen is a flat-roofed BR cabin dating back only to 1974. Blea Moor lies in very remote terrain and has no mains water supply; water used to be delivered by passing trains.

Many other great Midland-design boxes to be seen in this part of the country – such as at Skipton and on the Settle–Carnforth line – have now passed into history. Hellifield is one proud survivor but as things stand, it is scheduled to shut along with all boxes on the S&C in 2020. The main casualties will be: Howe & Co.'s Siding, Low House Crossing, Culgaith, Kirkby Thore (a twin-storey portakabin), Appleby North, Kirkby Stephen, Garsdale, Blea Moor and Settle Junction. Control of this route and the Cumbrian Coast will pass over to the new Manchester ROC.

The S&C has long been a favourite with photographers, though the weather across the Pennines is highly changeable. Unfortunately, it suffered badly from the storms of winter 2015/16, which caused a devastating landslide that blocked the line at Eden Brows, near Armathwaite, closing the route north of Appleby for several months. Trains have since been able to run north as far as Armathwaite only, with the line still severed at the time of writing, so much of the regular freight and charter traffic has been suspended. Network Rail is undertaking some major earthworks in the area to stop the same thing happening again and the full route is not expected to reopen until March 2017. To give an idea of the damage caused, this was reportedly the worst landslip on the S&C since the 1870s, when one at the same location took two years to rectify!

Blackpool North is one of very few sizeable terminuses in the country to retain semaphores but closure of the last remaining box there – Blackpool North No. 2 – is imminent. The Liverpool and Manchester areas retain a surprising number of boxes, controlling mostly colour light signals, which are due to shut between now and 2025, falling under the jurisdiction of Manchester ROC. Chester PSB is typical of those built by BR in the 1970s and 1980s, with an electrically operated NX panel installed to replace the mechanical lever frames in the old boxes it replaced. It is scheduled for replacement in 2024.

Helsby Junction holds one of only three surviving co-acting semaphore signals in the UK. There used to be many more of these, all provided in locations where a driver's view is restricted due to the signal being positioned directly behind an overbridge, footbridge or another obstacle, which means it cannot be seen until the last second. A duplicate arm is positioned higher up the signal post that copies the aspect of the lower one, meaning the driver can see from a distance whether or not it is clear and have more time to act accordingly.

Crewe still has a fascinating array of mechanical boxes centred around the goods 'independent' lines that avoid the station on the WCML, using Absolute Block methods but controlling colour lights. The use of such dated equipment on a busy, electrified section of line – not to mention giving access to several large depots and freight yards – is rare on today's railway. The boxes in question – Crewe Coal Yard, Salop Goods Junction, Gresty Lane No. 1, Crewe Sorting Sidings North and Basford Hall Junction – are to shut between 2020 and 2021. Control will transfer to another ROC, at Rugby.

Semaphores still dominate in the more rural areas in the North West such as the Peak District. Those on the Hope Valley line from Manchester to Sheffield are expected to be gone by 2020, while examples around Buxton and Peak Forest should hang on until 2025.

A Class 142 Pacer slows for the stop at Wigton on 10 March 2016 with 2C45, the 10.10 Barrow–Carlisle. The flat-roofed signal box added in 1957 is typical of those built by BR in the 1950s and 1960s. Carlisle power box controls the first 9½ miles of the Cumbrian Coast line north of here.

Ground disc shunt signals can still be seen almost everywhere where there is a manual box to control movements across points and into sidings. At least two of the examples seen here at Workington seem to be redundant as the fast lines through the station have been partially lifted, though the dismantled track has remained in place for some years.

Most large stations in the country used to have a signal box at either end. Workington is one of very few locations where this arrangement still exists. Main No. 3 box seen here controls the north end of the station and is a LNWR design.

At the other end of the station is Workington Main No. 2 (No. 1 box is no longer standing), seen on 10 March 2016 as heritage 'Large Logo' liveried Class 37 No. 37401 *Mary Queen of Scots* heads one of the daily loco-hauled Barrow–Carlisle services. Until recent years, there was considerable freight activity centred around the nearby steelworks.

A tranquil spring evening at the village station of Silecroft, with no sound to be heard but for nesting rooks in the trees. The level crossing has modern lifting barriers controlled manually from the Furness Railway (FR) box, which has been modernised with draught-proof uPVC windows like most others remaining on the network. The ground disc in the foreground is only likely to be used in emergencies for trains using the reverse crossover.

Limestone Hall level crossing near Silecroft lies in a magnificent setting beneath the fell of Black Combe and is watched over by a crossing keeper in a Portakabin who opens and closes the gates. On the far right, a six-lever frame can just be discerned, controlling the approach semaphores.

The lights are on at dusk inside Millom box. Unlike Silecroft, this timber-built cabin has had its downstairs locking room windows boarded over. A very early FR distant signal survived near here until the 1980s.

Above: Looking across Morecambe Bay at Arnside on 11 March 2016, as the No. 0831 Manchester Oxford Rd–Barrow passes. The Furness line's stone-built boxes such as this one (thirty-five levers) are among the finest in the country.

Right: Looking towards the Warcop branch junction at Appleby on the Settle & Carlisle line, with Appleby North box visible in the background. The main line connection is out of use, but the rest of the branch now forms the preserved Eden Valley Railway. Network Rail still retain a single-line staff for the 5½-mile route.

Preserved LMS Pacific No. 46229 *Duchess of Hamilton* leaves Garsdale following a water stop with a northbound special on 13 April 1990. The box, seen in the background, was switched out of use for much of the 1990s, but reopened after a rise in freight traffic. Garsdale was formerly the junction for Hawes. (David Webster)

Class 47 No. 47556 has a clear road ahead passing isolated Blea Moor on 3 April 1989 with a Leeds–Carlisle service. Still manned on 12-hour shifts, the box here remains an important outpost, as the Up goods loop is used for the recently started stone trains from Arcow Quarry to be run round. It also controls the start of the short single-line section to Ribblehead. (David Webster)

Settle Junction box is typical of Midland Railway designs seen on the Settle & Carlisle line and controls the junction where the route from Carnforth via Wennington joins. The section of the building sticking out on the far left is an annex containing a toilet, added in 2003 when the box was refurbished.

Hellifield is a formerly busy junction that is now eerily quiet, largely because the connection onto the Ribble Valley line to Blackburn (diverging on the far right) is sparsely used. The track seen to the left is the main line from Settle to Skipton and Leeds. The one surviving signal box is Hellifield South Junction – in steam days there were three around the station.

Hellifield does still retain an impressive array of semaphores, including shunt signals, seen here controlling the sidings and one of the goods loops. The one on the right is an exceptionally rare survivor, with a MR wooden post.

The scenic Hope Valley line from Sheffield to Manchester splits at New Mills South Junction, with the left fork leading to Stockport and the right direct to Manchester via Romiley. On 29 March 2016, First TransPennine Express No. 185139 heads for Stockport. The box is another MR design and also controls an Up goods loop, the rusty line at the bottom right of the picture.

Romiley Junction box, on the outskirts of Manchester, closed in 2014 and was still standing on this visit two years later, looking rather forlorn with its windows boarded up. Its MR origins are not so obvious; it is a Type 2b design dating back to 1899 but heavily modified, with uPVC windows added latterly.

Peak Forest South box controls access to a quarry and holding sidings that are part of DB Cargo's freight depot, housed in the old station building. On 29 March 2016, Class 66s Nos 66105 (shunting, left) and 66013 (on the fuelling road) are seen at work.

Half a mile to the south is Great Rocks Junction box, which with its flat roof looks like a BR design. It was in fact opened in 1923, the year the MR became part of the LMS, but has since been re-roofed, re-windowed and given a new coat of green and cream paint in common with other boxes in the Peak District. It guards the entrance to Tunstead quarry beside the Chinley–Buxton line.

Helsby Junction is where trains for Ellesmere Port and Hooton diverge from the Warrington–Chester main line. The station is beautifully kept by volunteers and their list of awards is proudly displayed on the left-hand side of this 1900-vintage LNWR box, refurbished in 2002. The quality of the restoration won it the Westinghouse Signalling Award in 2004, as denoted on the plaque at the front.

At Helsby there is also an extremely rare co-acting signal where the Hooton line joins, seen on the left as No. 67002 propels a Holyhead–Manchester Piccadilly service away on April Fool's Day 2016. It is so called as it has two arms that both display the same aspect. The extra upper arm is provided to aid visibility, as the driver's view is restricted by the station footbridge immediately in front of it.

Wartime austerity is evident in the appearance of Crewe Coal Yard box, opened in 1939 by the LMS. Standing adjacent to the WCML, it is one of several boxes that remain operational in Crewe, a town still dominated by large marshalling yards and depots. By 2021, the area will be controlled by Rugby ROC.

CHAPTER 2

North East

The North Eastern Railway (NER) was one of the dominating railway companies in Great Britain prior to the 1923 Grouping when it became part of the London & North Eastern Railway (LNER), one of the 'Big Four'. The NER had the lion's share of control in Yorkshire and Northumberland and also some of the best-designed signal boxes. A significant number of them are still around on the main line today and as the following pages show, there were many variations in design and construction material, though all are very photogenic.

Some great examples survive on the lines serving Scarborough from both Hull and York, and current plans suggest they will stay in use until 2026, meaning they may be some of the last boxes in the country to close. Those on the Hull route are at Beverley, Driffield and Bridlington South, while there is a gate box at Gristhorpe. On the York route there is Strensall, Barton Hill, Kirkham Abbey, Malton, Weaverthorpe and Howsham gate box, while Seamer is positioned at the junction where both routes join outside Scarborough. Current traffic consists mainly of diesel multiple units (DMUs) so the lines have not attracted a great deal of photographic attention, though the steam-hauled Scarborough Spa Expresses provide interest, running from York in the summer months. The now-disused Falsgrave box at Scarborough station had a magnificent semaphore gantry until it was closed in 2010. Happily, the gantry has been relocated to Grosmont on the preserved North Yorkshire Moors Railway.

The York–Harrogate line truly is the land that time forgot in north-east England, with Victorian infrastructure dominating throughout its twenty-mile length. The main boxes are at Harrogate, Starbeck, Knaresborough, Cattal, Hammerton and Poppleton (closing 2018). Manual gated level crossings are still in operation at most of these stations *plus* another five sites in between where a crossing keeper is still stationed to open and close the gates on what are mostly quiet country roads.

Brass Key Tokens control access for the Knaresborough–Cattal and Hammerton–Poppleton single track sections. Taking Cattal as an example, before allowing a train to head west, the signaller must obtain permission (via a bell code) from his/her colleague at Knaresborough box to signify that the line ahead is clear, as they would on double track using Absolute Block. They are then able to release the section token from the instrument in the box and the token is then handed to the train's driver. At Knaresborough, the driver surrenders the token, which the signaller there places in the corresponding instrument for that section. The apparatus will only allow one token to be released for a particular section at any one time; another cannot be physically removed from the machine until the first one is placed back in.

The Middlesbrough-Whitby Esk Valley line uses No Signaller Token Remote arrangements, whereby train crews are required to physically release and return the Key Tokens from the instruments themselves. This occurs during stops at Battersby, Glaisdale and Whitby, where they do it under instructions from the signaller at Nunthorpe box (closing 2017) to swap tokens from the secure cabinets at the stations. As there are instruments at multiple locations with unattended crossing loops, this method differs from the No Signaller Key Token working examined later. Other boxes on Teeside closing in 2017 are Bowesfield, Tees Yard, Middlesbrough, Whitehouse, Grangetown, Redcar, Long Beck and Crag Hall. Joining them in the history books three years later will be the boxes on the NER's Tyne Valley line from Newcastle to Carlisle.

The state-of-the-art York ROC will become the sole control point for virtually the whole of north-east England, including the East Coast Main Line, after the last mechanical boxes shut. Its massive area of jurisdiction will stretch right down from Tyneside to Lincolnshire, covering the former territories of both the North Eastern and Great Central Railway companies.

One of the most recent transfers to York came during the North Lincolnshire re-signalling project of Christmas 2015. Before this, an incredible variety of semaphores and mechanical boxes could still be found in Humberside. The most notable location was Barnetby station, which became a Mecca for photographers latterly, due to the intense volume of freight passing between the boxes at Barnetby East and Wrawby Junction. Also expected to close shortly are boxes on the Selby–Hull line; at Gilberdyke Junction, Broomfleet, Crabley Creek, Brough East and Melton Lane, plus the gate boxes at Oxmardyke, Cave and Welton.

Barnetby station's appearance would be changed forever just over a month after this view on 12 November 2015, with special Tata Steel-liveried No. 60099 passing the East box on the 6D31 Lindsey–West Burton oil tankers. Trackside workers were in abundance throughout that day, probably as preparation work for the decommissioning of the semaphores, part of the North Lincolnshire re-signalling project.

Until December 2015, Wrawby Junction box, at the opposite end of Barnetby station, controlled the important three-way junction for the lines west to Lincoln, Gainsborough and Scunthorpe. On 12 November 2015, No. 66007 passes the doomed semaphores with a biomass working.

A general view of Barnetby's west end, showing a rural location dominated by the railway. No. 153313 is on the 09.57 Newark North Gate–Grimsby Town, passing a coal train and signal BE49 on the left. The distant arm would give drivers warning if the junction stop signal was set at 'danger' and appeared in latter days to be permanently fixed at 'caution'.

Right: This rare semaphore – with a lattice post and wooden supporting dolls – stood the test of time at Barnetby until re-signalling at Christmas 2015.

Below: The splendid 1910-built Great Central Railway (GCR) box at Ulceby Junction controlled both semaphores and colour lights before it was sadly demolished in January 2016. Two months before the end, Colas Rail's No. 60096 approaches on a Preston Docks–Lindsey oil working. The lines pictured are at one end of a triangle allowing movements in the direction of either Cleethorpes (left) or Barnetby (right).

We are now looking, a few minutes later, in the other direction from the box, towards Ulceby North Junction, where the lines to Barton-on-Humber and Immingham separate. The driver of No. 60010 blasts the horn to warn nearby track workers as he comes off the latter route. There are more than 260 freight movements a day at Immingham docks.

Brocklesby Junction box formerly controlled another end of the Barnetby–Ulceby–Cleethorpes triangle. Not long before its closure, in the dying light of 12 November 2015, DB Schenker-liveried No. 66118 comes off the line from Ulceby with an empty steel train. The disused station pictured shut as late as October 1993, and both the main building and box are still standing as they are Grade II listed.

North of the Humber, time is running out for boxes on the Selby–Hull line, including that at Gilberdyke Junction (formerly known as Staddlethorpe Junction). A storm is brewing as Class 144 Pacer No. 144009 approaches from the east on 13 November 2015. It has just passed a coal train, seen in the distance.

Northern Rail's No. 158844 joins the main line from the adjoining Goole and Doncaster route at Gilberdyke on 13 November 2015. As well as the 'fishtail' distant semaphore arms (both still working) note the left-hand signal has a sighting board behind the stop arm to make it more visible to drivers.

Beverley box on the Hull–Scarborough route is a typically handsome NER structure from 1911, with a McKenzie & Holland frame holding twenty levers. It has an important function controlling a level crossing on a busy main road though colour light signals are now in abundance.

The one surviving box at Bridlington (Bridlington South) makes for an impressive sight as No. 158791 passes on a service from Hull. It is one of five boxes to survive between Hull and Scarborough, and its size harks back to bygone days of summer excursion trains when the track layout was far more extensive. Traffic on the line today is more or less just a steady stream of Northern Rail DMUs.

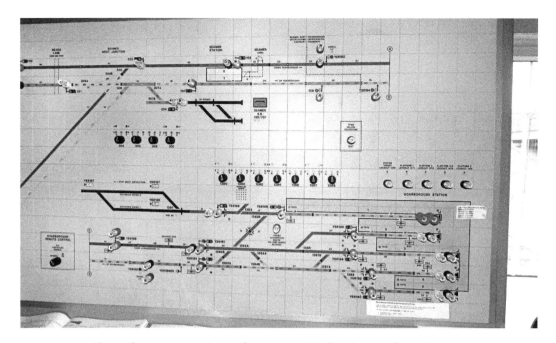

Seamer (formerly Seamer East) is a classic 1910 NER box but inside is this NX panel installed during re-signalling in 2000. This view shows its control of the junction and, below, Scarborough station. (Nick Jones, permission of Network Rail)

At Malton, there is one of eighty-nine level crossings (either supervised or user-worked) on the 42-mile York–Scarborough line, overlooked by another NER box, which is in excellent order. There are four roads that converge here, which looks potentially dangerous. Until 1965, a line from Pickering joined at nearby Rillington Junction, now the missing link on the preserved North Yorkshire Moors Railway.

Kirkham Abbey level crossing lies in beautiful Yorkshire countryside and still has wooden gates that are wheel-operated. House martins nest under the eaves of the 1873 Grade II-listed box, which won a National Railway Heritage award in 2011. (Nick Jones)

The crossing gate wheel inside Kirkham Abbey box, one of very few left in Britain. There are just eight operational levers in the frame, with only one stop signal in the Down direction (towards Scarborough). It is more common to see at least two: a 'Home' and a 'Starter'. (Nick Jones, permission of Network Rail)

Semaphore gantries were once a common sight at major stations but are now few and far between. This one at Harrogate has survived, albeit scaled back, and carries a shunt arm on the left.

Harrogate box (formerly Harrogate North) is an austere LNER flat-roofed design from 1947, holding forty-five levers. Until 1981, there was a second box controlling the south end of the station.

Modern barrier crossings are actually in the minority on the York–Harrogate route at the time of writing. The 1915 NER box at Starbeck station (twenty-six levers), on the outskirts of Harrogate, guards one of them.

Knaresborough box is uniquely attached to a row of houses and controls one of the many manual gated level crossings on the York–Harrogate route. Also of note is the reverse crossover and the Down bracket starting signal located on the Up side. But for the second generation DMUs on show (Classes 144 and 150), it could easily be a scene from the 1950s!

Whixley crossing is one of several countryside gate boxes on the York–Harrogate line. The gates across the minor farm road were very recently upgraded from the wooden originals and are closed to vehicles until a driver approaches and uses a plunger to alert the crossing keeper, who is based inside the Portakabin.

The diminutive box and level crossing at Cattal marks the start of a short double-track section or 'dynamic loop' towards Hammerton on the Harrogate–York route. No. 150269 rolls in off the single line on 11 November 2015 with a Harrogate service. Knaresborough to Cattal – which uses Key Token working – was singled in December 1973.

The end of the double-track section at Hammerton station, with yet another gated crossing. Note the elderly wooden gates from this view on a very mild 11 November 2015.

The view west from Hammerton station, looking towards York. There is no signal box here; the ten-lever frame is located in a platform cupboard, with block instruments in the station building. The distant protects Wilstrop occupation crossing and is always set 'off' during daytime hours except for when the gates are opened for a vehicle to cross.

A Class 150 Sprinter approaches Wilstrop crossing. A crossing keeper is based here to control a five-lever frame that is housed inside a bus shelter-type structure just visible on the left.

A modern-built 'traditional' box at Low Row on the Tyne Valley line from Carlisle to Newcastle. It was constructed in 2009 to replace the original NER structure that was located on the opposite side of the line. The last remaining boxes on this route control a mixture of semaphores and colour lights and are planned to close in 2020.

The signals are off in both directions at Haydon Bridge on 14 November 2015, as Northern Rail's No. 156454 arrives, passing the immaculate 1877-built box. The original wooden, wheel-operated crossing gates were replaced in January 2009 with the automatic barriers seen here.

The NER boxes at Hexham and Wylam are both spectacular Grade II-listed structures that straddle the running lines. At the former, a busy scene on 14 November 2015 sees Sprinter No. 156481 leave for Newcastle as a Virgin HST thunders past on a London King's Cross–Edinburgh service, diverted due to engineering work on the East Coast Main Line.

The North Eastern must have liked a box with a view! On 14 November 2015, No. 67026 *Diamond Jubilee* sweeps through Prudhoe with a Class 91 electric in tow on the 0650 Glasgow Central–King's Cross, diverted from the East Coast Main Line. The adjacent single-track road bridge over the River Tyne was closed for refurbishment during this period; normally, it causes considerable traffic queues at the level crossing.

No. 142026 departs Wylam with the No. 0943 Hexham–Nunthorpe, passing under the box that was refurbished in 2003 with the support of the Railway Heritage Trust. Beside it is the Boathouse, 'Arguably the best pub in the world' according to its sign!

CHAPTER 3

Scotland

A large proportion of Scotland is still controlled by mechanical boxes at the time of writing, though it is generally split between two areas: the north-east and south-west. Mass re-signalling took place in the 1980s but before this, semaphores ruled almost everywhere but for Glasgow, Edinburgh, and the West and East Coast Main Lines.

One such project was the Glasgow–Ayr/Largs/Ardrossan electrification, which resulted in closure of all boxes along these routes between 1986 and 1989. South of Girvan on the single line to Stranraer there is seemingly a time warp, as this is the last part of the British Rail network to feature Electric Token Block working using tablets. These are still exchanged in traditional fashion between signaller and driver with the tablet contained in a pouch on a metal hoop for ease of handling, with the only difference being that trains are now required to stop for the exchange. There are tales aplenty from the line when the tokens used to be swapped at speed!

Tyer's No. 6 tablet instruments remain for this purpose at Dunragit, Glenwhilly, Barrhill and Girvan. Being built earlier, they are much bulkier than Key Token machines. The boxes at these locations, together with Stranraer Harbour (currently switched out) and Kilkerran (Tokenless Block), are scheduled to close in 2021. Crossing loops on the line were extended during the Second World War when it became busy with military traffic, in order to handle double-headed trains of up to twelve coaches. Signal positions were altered as a result.

Ayrshire still has a few freight-only branch lines, the remnants of a once vast network of mineral railways. Invariably, lightly used routes like these use simple One Train Working arrangements, which as it sounds, only allows a single train to use the whole line at any one time. Upon entering one of these branches, a driver will collect a brass token or staff (a baton-like instrument made of wood or metal), which will give their train sole occupation of the line until they leave the route and hand it back, at which point it becomes available for the next train. The steeply graded line to Killoch colliery uses One Train Working with a staff. This is retrieved from a locked cabinet at Annbank Junction, where it leaves the main Ayr–Mauchline route, as there is no signal box there.

Another interesting switchback branch to use the staff-based method is Dalrymple Junction–Chalmerston, the former route to Dalmellington. It has been out of use for a few years however. Dunragit–Stranraer uses the same method as Stranraer Harbour box is not usually open. The short line to Greenburn opencast mine diverges from the Glasgow & South Western Railway (GSWR) main line at Bank Junction, just north of New Cumnock, and uses One Train Working but without any form of token or staff, though access is controlled by the signaller at New Cumnock, where there is a One Control Switch (OCS) panel. Interestingly, the Greenburn line was part of an old industrial railway that had been abandoned for decades, before Network Rail re-laid the track in 2004 for regular coal workings. However, trains have become sporadic recently following the decline of the domestic coal market and the branch, along with that to Killoch, will probably be mothballed.

The Ayr–Mauchline freight-only route could also end up disused for the same reasons. There is a signal box at one end only: Mauchline (built 1877, thirty-five levers), where it joins the GSWR main line. As a result, No Signaller Key Token working is in operation, with a cabinet located near its westernmost extremity that was formerly known as Blackhouse Junction, Ayr. The Mauchline signaller gives drivers permission via phone to remove a token from the cabinet, though the colour light signal here is controlled by the West of Scotland Signalling Centre (WSSC), Cowlairs, along with the Glasgow–Ayr line. Trains for Killoch have to collect a token heading east and then give it up at Annbank Junction.

The GSWR main line from Glasgow to Carlisle has been busy with passenger and freight traffic in recent years, with occasional diversions from the WCML to boot. However, the loss of much coal traffic in the past couple of years has produced much longer gaps between trains. The line also still uses GSWR Absolute Block instruments for much of its 115-mile length. The remaining boxes at Annan, Dumfries, Holywood, Thornhill, Kirkconnel, New Cumnock, Mauchline, Hurlford (switched out), Kilmarnock, Lugton and Barrhead are to close in 2023–24.

Control of the Scottish network will eventually be split between two ROCs: Glasgow and Edinburgh (near Waverley station). Glasgow ROC is to take over from the signalling centres at Motherwell and Yoker from 2017–22. It is being developed as an expansion of the existing WSSC at Cowlairs, which currently controls much of Glasgow and south-west Scotland. The West Highland Lines to Oban, Fort William and Mallaig will eventually be taken over by Edinburgh ROC in 2040; until then they will continue to use the Radio Electronic Token Block (RETB) technology adopted in 1988. Though there is still one remaining manual box: Fort William Junction (formerly named Mallaig Junction), which still controls the yards and station at Fort William (closing 2025).

Semaphores are also still extant in the Pass of Brander on the Oban line, though these are independently controlled by a unique trip wire system to warn drivers of rockfalls. There are seventeen signals altogether, spaced at quarter-mile intervals, with all but two possessing bi-directional twin arms. They are set to show a permanent 'clear' aspect, unless a rock or any hillside debris breaks the trip wires in which case they drop to 'danger'. The system was invented by John Anderson, secretary of the Callander & Oban Railway, during 1882. It was noticed that the trip wires produced an odd musical sound with the wind blowing, thus the section of line soon gained the nickname 'Anderson's Piano'. An accident black spot ever since the early days of the railway, a landslide here in 2010 saw a ScotRail train derail and almost plunge down a 50-foot embankment on to the road below. Network Rail recently trialled new protective fibre-optic cables at the location, which, if successful, could spell the end for the semaphores.

In the mid-1980s, the Inverness–Kyle of Lochalsh/Wick/Thurso lines also went from mechanical to RETB signalling, though Clachnaharry box near Inverness (expected to survive until 2035) is still in place to control a swing bridge on the Caledonian Canal, similar to the RETB signalling centre at Banavie on the West Highland Extension line. South of Inverness, the Highland main line to Perth is the classic example of the Scottish region Tokenless Block system in action. This involves single-line working without tokens or any form of train detection such as track circuits, but with electrically activated cabinets in the signal boxes to allow signallers to give word of trains entering and leaving sections, thereby allowing high speed running. The Inverness to Kingussie section uses TCB working instead. The boxes at Aviemore, Kingussie, Dalwhinnie, Blair Atholl, Pitlochry, Dunkeld and Stanley Junction are to close from 2021 to 2024. Most of them are small structures that have had sizeable extensions added in recent years.

Tokenless Block is also found on the Inverness–Aberdeen route, which is single-track bar for a 6-mile double section from Insch to Kennethmont. Forres–Nairn still uses Key Tokens and the instrument for these inside Nairn station building is unusually paired with a modern Westcad VDU screen controlling the 14 miles west to Inverness. Before re-signalling in April 2000, it was the last station on the Highland Railway (HR) network with a working box at either end and the signalman would run down the platform between them on a bicycle to work the levers! The Aberdeen to Inverness Rail Improvements scheme – a long-term project between now and 2030 – will see track redoubling from Aberdeen to Inverurie and a realignment at Forres, not to mention the abolition of all surviving boxes. In the case of Nairn, Forres, Inverurie and Dyce this could be as early as 2016, with those at Elgin West, Keith, Huntly, Kennethmont and Insch to soldier on until 2024.

The northern extension of the East Coast Main Line from Dundee to Aberdeen is a traditional main line if ever there was one, with 100 mph running in places and semaphores virtually throughout. Indeed, over the whole route from Aberdeen to Stirling via Perth there are no less than nineteen boxes, many at closed stations, retained to control level crossings and to break the line into shorter block sections. Most north of Dundee should survive until 2024; namely Newtonhill, Stonehaven, Carmont, Laurencekirk, Craigo, Montrose North, Inverkeilor and Arbroath. Carnoustie is expected to shut between 2016 and 2017, along with Errol, Longforgan, Barnhill (Perth), Perth power box, Hilton Junction, Auchterarder, Blackford, Greenloaning, Dunblane, Stirling North and Stirling Middle.

Completing the picture of forthcoming box closures in east-central Scotland will be Carmuirs East, Larbert North and Grangemouth Junction (all closing 2016), then Dundee Signalling Centre, Tay Bridge South, Leuchars, Cupar, Longannet and Fouldubs Junction (2025). One of the most fascinating locations used to be the Larbert triangle, which still had semaphores and a box at each corner until colour lights were installed in 2007.

Also worth mentioning is the abundance of boxes in Scotland that were designed by independent signalling contractors, rather than the railway companies. This is most typical of earlier designs, when companies like the Highland Railway utilised the services of McKenzie & Holland for example, before developing their own style. All over the UK there are numerous examples of McKenzie & Holland boxes to be seen, together with those of other major contractors like Saxby & Farmer, and it is interesting to note the similarity between them, for example, Kingussie box and Tutbury in Derbyshire, despite their vastly different regions. Kingussie, Blair Atholl, Aviemore, Forres, and Clachnaharry are all McKenzie & Holland design, while Kennethmont was designed by the Railway Signal Co.

As remote locations go, Glenwhilly is surely in a league of its own. Lying amid a windswept moor on the Ayr–Stranraer line, with nothing but scattered farms for miles in either direction, it closed as a station in 1965 but still survives today as a crossing loop. On 21 October 2015, the No. 1443 Stranraer–Kilmarnock accelerates away, having stopped for the signaller and driver to exchange the single-line tablet.

A flashback to 26 September 1988 sees Class 47 No. 47604 *Woman's Royal Voluntary Service* heading the No. 1223 Glasgow Central–Stranraer service, past the Glenwhilly Down distant signal at Marklach farm crossing. (David Webster)

The same signal at Glenwhilly, still there in 2016 and now the last surviving distant semaphore in Scotland. It is, however, motorised, so the signaller no longer has a mile-long length of wire to pull!

The tiny box at Barrhill – the only intermediate station between Girvan and Stranraer – has an eighteen-lever frame, but the tablet instruments are located in the station building. This October 2015 view shows No. 156508 awaiting the passage of a southbound service.

Above: The afternoon Stranraer–Tees Yard freight enters Barrhill on 26 September 1988, with no less than three locos at the helm; No. 47157 is leading No. 37009 and No. 47152. Note the driver about to swap the tablet. Triple-headed workings are rare enough (and more often than not for positioning purposes) but photographs of any involved in a tablet exchange must be very few and far between. (David Webster)

Right: A close-up of the Tyer's No. 6 tablet instrument still in use in Girvan box, actually a replacement machine added in 1991 following the closure of Pinwherry box and the extension of the block section south through to Barrhill. Unusually, it is at the north (Kilkerran) end of the box, while the Tokenless Block controls for the section to Kilkerran are at the Barrhill end. Signalman Stuart Scott is in the background. (Nick Jones, permission of Network Rail)

Kilkerran, between Girvan and Ayr, closed as a station in 1965, but its GSWR box survives to control the crossing loop and level crossing. The box is timber-built and typical of GSWR construction, now refurbished with a toilet and the usual refinements such as insulated uPVC windows.

New Cumnock on the Glasgow & South Western main line. A Saturday of diversions from the West Coast route via Beattock, on 20 March 2004, sees a southbound Virgin 'Super Voyager' passing under the semaphores. Class 57/3 No. 57312 *The Hood* idles in the coal terminal siding, based here as a standby loco in case of failures. It would see action later in the day. (David Webster)

No. 156508 arrives at Kirkconnel (opened 1911, forty-two levers) on 31 July 2014. The bushes on the right cover what used to be colliery sidings. GSWR Absolute Block instruments are still used to hand trains over towards the boxes north at New Cumnock and south at Thornhill.

The last wheel-operated level crossing in Scotland – and one of just a small number in Britain – is at Holywood, just north of Dumfries. It is pictured in March 2004, a few years after the GSWR box had been given a welcome facelift by Railtrack. The red, painted-over brickwork is typical of many refurbished Scottish boxes and note how the small outbuilding to the left has also been treated!

Above: Unusual semaphores survive in the Pass of Brander near Loch Awe as part of a unique system conceived back in 1882 by the Callander & Oban Railway to warn drivers of rockfalls. They are connected to a wire screen (pictured in foreground) which, if broken by a boulder, will cause the signal arms to fall to danger. No. 156457 passes on 30 October 2015.

Left: Fort William Junction box controls some fine lattice post semaphores where the Mallaig and Glasgow lines converge, as well as the short Track Circuit Block section from there to Fort William station using colour lights. On 6 July 2015, Black Five No. 45407 passes Inverlochy, having taken the Mallaig route with the 'Jacobite' steam service.

The largest working box in Scotland is Stirling Middle, a superb 1900 Caledonian Railway (CR) brick-built design with a ninety-six-lever frame. Note the bay window, provided to give the signaller a better view down towards the station. Stirling is the last station north of the border to be controlled by a box at either end. Both controlled a great sea of lattice post semaphores until most were removed in October 2013 and replaced by colour lights.

At the other side of the station, Stirling North box is also impressive, seen here on 16 September 2015 with No. 158728 arriving. It is essentially a shorter version of its neighbour, holding a forty-eight-lever frame, and was commissioned in 1901. To the left is one of the very few remaining semaphore signals. The route to Longannet power station and Alloa (reopened to passenger trains in 2008) diverges from the main line to Perth here.

Left: A northbound Turbostar unit is seen at Greenloaning on a very warm 16 September 2015, passing Scotland's last co-acting semaphore signal on the left. The box is normally switched out of use these days; hence why both signals are 'off'.

Below: On the same afternoon as the last picture, the weather has now taken a turn for the worse as the London King's Cross–Inverness 'Highland Chieftain' sweeps through Blackford. The old goods yard here is to be reopened as a modern container-handling terminal for Highland Spring water, by which time the signal box will likely be closed.

The temperature is barely above freezing on the morning of 25 February 2016, as a pair of ScotRail Class 158s speed over Errol level crossing on a Glasgow–Dundee service. The ex-Caledonian box at this now-closed station, built in 1877, is Grade B listed. The lattice post signal appears to be in good order as well.

Longforgan box (twenty levers), showing the contrasting styles that can be found on the Perth–Dundee route. It has a distinctive bay window, being one of a handful of pre-war LMS designs north of the border. Others in this style are at Blackford, Lugton, Dunragit and Hurlford.

1S11, the 10.00 King's Cross–Aberdeen HST, accelerates out of Arbroath on 24 February 2016, passing the distinctive truss-supported box and its level crossing. The box had windows stretching almost the whole way round until some were plated over in recent years.

Amazingly, Network Rail has erected new semaphore signals in recent years at the odd location. These two examples at Montrose were added in 2009, when the Up line became bi-directional through the station. Montrose North box, pictured, was reopened after a spell switched out, while those at Montrose South and Usan were closed and knocked down as part of the same re-signalling scheme.

Craigo box was recently switched out, resulting in a block section of over 10 miles from Montrose to Laurencekirk, but it can be reopened as and when required. On 24 February 2016, the 1E25 14.52 Aberdeen–King's Cross HST meets pioneer Class 68 No. 68001 *Evolution* on the 4A13 12.23 Grangemouth–Aberdeen Craiginches freight.

Turbostar No. 170459 speeds non-stop through Laurencekirk on its way to Aberdeen. Note how quickly the signal nearest the camera has returned to danger. Laurencekirk station reopened in 2009 and the goods yard was used in recent years for pipe traffic.

The Perth–Inverness Highland main line is largely single track using the Scottish Tokenless Block system. At Dunkeld, there is a surviving platform formerly used for the signalman to exchange tokens by hand. Also note the superb tall signal, controlling the Up loop, which retains its HR finial.

Pitlochry is a 1911 HR box; refurbished after privatisation (with a rear extension) and Grade A listed along with the station. At 7.30 p.m. on 6 July 2015, Freightliner Class 66 No. 66619 *Derek W. Johnson MBE* passes with No. 6B31, the weekly No. 1759 Inverness–Oxwellmains cement empties.

Dalwhinnie, the highest operational signal box in Britain, at approximately 1,160 feet above sea level, built by the HR in 1909. No. 170428 passes non-stop on the evening of 6 July 2015, heading south off the single line on to the 24-mile double-track section to Blair Atholl over Druimuachdar Summit. Note the old water tower base.

The largest remaining box on HR territory is at Aviemore, and it will be 125 years old when it is scheduled to close in 2023. The preserved Strathspey Railway diverges from the Perth–Inverness route, as seen here with Ivatt 2MT No. 46512 arriving from Boat of Garten in 2015. Its thirty-lever frame does not control the heritage line, which has its own box just out of the picture, relocated from Garve on the Kyle of Lochalsh line.

Elgin West, the most northerly working signal box in Britain. It controls a level crossing and the present HR-built station, formerly known itself as Elgin West. Until 1968, Elgin East station lay adjacent, and there were another two boxes in its vicinity, one of which (Elgin Centre) still stands but is slowly crumbling apart next to the goods yard.

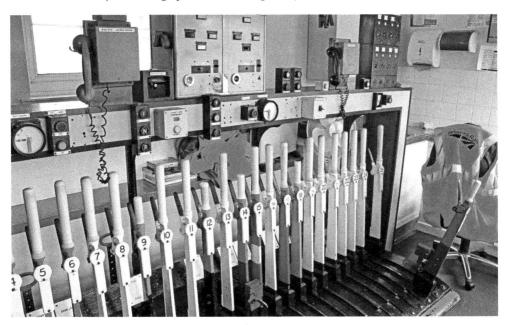

Elgin West's twenty-six-lever frame. The red levers control stop signals, the yellows distants, blues point locks and the whites are those no longer in use. The blue cabinets above the frame are for Tokenless Block working. The one on the left is used to pass trains to or from Keith, but the one on the right is not in use, as trains west to Forres use key tokens. A token for access to the Burghead branch, which has been mothballed and overgrown for some years, is still in the box. (Author, permission of Network Rail)

Keith Junction box and its forty-lever frame, pictured mid-afternoon on 20 June 2015 as the signallers were changing shift. The connecting branch to Dufftown closed in 1991 but this is now preserved as the Keith & Dufftown Railway, but for a short section of lifted track near here that has disconnected it from the Inverness–Aberdeen main line. (Author, permission of Network Rail)

Huntly box is heavily refurbished and unrecognisable from its previous incarnation as Huntly South gate box. The neighbouring North box closed in 1970, so this became the cabin controlling the whole station. Like many other stations on the Inverness–Aberdeen route, the semaphore-controlled loop is bi-directional. (Author, permission of Network Rail)

CHAPTER 4

Wales and Borders

There is some real variation in signalling methods to be found in Wales today, and this includes the new ETCS that has been piloted by Network Rail on the Cambrian line to Aberystwyth and Pwllheli. This was fully introduced in 2010, replacing the RETB system of the 1980s. Another lengthy cross-country route – the Heart of Wales line from Craven Arms to Llanelli – uses No Signaller Token Remote working, which like RETB brought considerable savings when it was introduced by BR in 1986.

A significant mileage of the Welsh network is still covered by mechanical boxes and semaphores using Absolute Block, including three of the trunk routes. The North Wales Coast line from Chester to Holyhead has a significant number of historical boxes now listed by Cadw, all still in use at the time of writing, though many are doomed to be closed within months possibly. The length of their tenure on this fast, inter-city route has been remarkable, going back to the days of the London & North Western Railway (LNWR). In 1923, the line became the LMS's main artery into Wales, which was largely Great Western Railway (GWR) territory, the most famous express train being the Irish Mail from London Euston to Holyhead. Similar 'boat trains' continue today from the capital city, run by Virgin, for ferry connections to Ireland.

All boxes east of Llandudno Junction on the North Wales Coast were planned for closure at the time of going to print in 2016, but it looks likely that re-signalling may now be pushed back until the following year. Those due for replacement are Rockcliffe Hall (Portakabin), Holywell Junction, Mostyn, Talacre, Prestatyn, Rhyl and Abergele and Pensarn. Also closing will be those on the double-track Llandudno branch: Llandudno station and Deganwy. The boxes further west out to Anglesey, at Llandudno Junction, Penmaenmawr, Bangor, Llanfair PG (gate box), Gaerwen, Ty Croes (gate box), Valley and Holyhead, should join them in 2020, as will Llanrwst on the Blaenau Ffestiniog branch. Control will become the responsibility of Cardiff ROC, which will look after the whole of Wales. At present, the Blaenau branch still uses Key Token working, with a 'No Signaller' variant south of Llanrwst.

Manual boxes along the Welsh Marches route from Newport to Shrewsbury will join Cardiff ROC in 2017. These are at Little Mill Junction, Abergavenny, Pontrilas, Tram Inn, Hereford, Moreton-on-Lugg, Leominster, Woofferton Junction, Bromfield, Onibury, Craven Arms, Marshbrook and Dorrington. On the line north to Chester, Gobowen North and

Croes Newydd should remain operational until 2025, along with those at Penyffordd and Dee Marsh Junction heading across the border towards Birkenhead.

The No Signaller Token Remote working (as mentioned earlier on the Middlesbrough-Whitby route) on the Heart of Wales line is controlled from the one remaining box at Pantyffynnon (closing 2020). Heading south onto the South Wales main line at Llanelli, more conventional signalling dominates on the double track out west to the coast, with boxes at Pembrey, Kidwelly, Ferryside, Carmarthen Junction, Whitland and Clarbeston Road (2022). Attractive GWR lower quadrant semaphores survive in many spots, though there's no such luck in the Welsh Valleys anymore, where Cardiff ROC is tightening its grip. Other boxes closing around the region include Newport Park Junction (2017) and Bishton (2019), which survives as a gate box only to control the Western region's last remaining wheel-operated level crossing, across a quadruple-track section of the South Wales main line.

At the time of going to press, the area with the largest concentration of semaphore signalling in the UK is Shrewsbury, which has four working boxes within a mile radius. Just across the border from Wales, several main lines meet at the town's 1848-built station, which lies in the shadow of Shrewsbury Castle in a meander of the River Severn. A plethora of lower and upper quadrant semaphores are controlled by a box at each end, guarding access across some complex pointwork to complete this historical scene. The boxes alone are hugely impressive; Severn Bridge Junction is the largest in the world and houses 180 levers. Dimensions-wise, it is 38 feet tall, 11 feet wide and 95 feet long, and has been known to shake when the wind is blowing strongly! Together with the neighbouring boxes Crewe Junction, Abbey Foregate and Sutton Bridge Junction, it has been Grade II listed by English Heritage in advance of closure in 2025.

GWR-era signalling also still prevails in Worcestershire. Well worth a visit are the boxes at Worcester Shrub Hill, Worcester Tunnel Junction, Droitwich Spa, Henwick, Newland East, Malvern Wells and Ledbury (planned for closure in 2020).

The end is nigh for the semaphores along the North Wales Coast line, with all boxes east of Llandudno Junction set to close shortly after going to print. Class 175 No. 175113 passes the closed station of Holywell Junction on 1 April 2016, with the derelict ex-BR passenger vessel *Duke of Lancaster* seen in the background, beached at Mostyn docks since 1979.

Approaching in the other direction is Class 67 No. 67002 with an Arriva Trains Wales service bound for Holyhead. Note the signal arms are carried on a bracket sticking out from the post, a common sight nowadays. Usually, these exist to improve sighting for drivers, possibly the case here being at the end of a curve, though there was clearly an extra arm carried on the right side of the signal at one point.

Mostyn box is another one normally 'switched out', that is, left unmanned with the signals cleared, meaning for all intents and purposes it does not exist. The block section therefore normally runs for 6 miles from Holywell Junction to Talacre. On 1 April 2016, No. 175101 races past Mostyn on the 11.44 Llandudno–Manchester Airport, beneath a neat little gantry.

The twenty-four-lever box at Talacre formerly controlled the entrance to Point of Ayr colliery (closed in 1996) on the most northerly point of mainland Wales. The disused and rusted connecting line can be seen on the right, while beyond the bridge is an abandoned platform of the station, which shut in 1966.

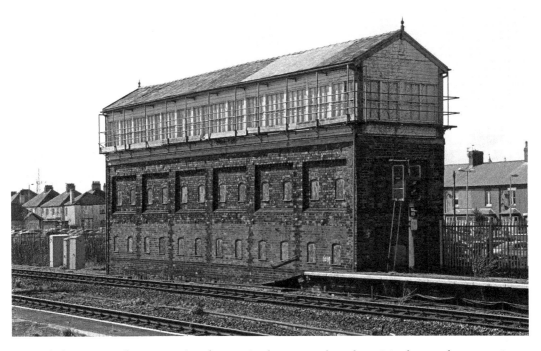

Rhyl station underwent major changes in the 1990s when the original semaphore gantries at either end were replaced. No. 2 box seen here, at the west end, closed in 1990 but is Grade II listed and still stands, albeit not in great condition.

The slightly smaller Rhyl No. 1 box (ninety levers) controls the remaining semaphores and colour lights at the station. Like its big brother, the great height gives the signaller an ideal grandstand view of trains passing to and from the platforms. On 31 March 2016, the 12.32 Holyhead–Maesteg service leaves the station.

1D35, the 10.36 Manchester Airport–Llandudno Junction, arrives at Abergele and Pensarn on 31 March 2016. The semaphores are tubular post examples, as are the majority remaining on the network. BR swore by this design, installing them in place of large amounts of pre-Grouping company signals (many lower quadrant) during the 1950s and 1960s.

Despite track rationalisation, Abergele station retains a fast line for Down trains running non-stop. A Class 175 Coradia DMU leaves for Manchester Airport on 31 March 2016, passing the soon-to-close LNWR box, which has sixty levers. Point rodding is visible alongside the track and wires connecting the semaphores can also just be made out behind it.

Penmaenmawr box is an uncompromising brick-built structure from 1952, derived from wartime 'Big Four' company designs (like Crewe Coal Yard seen earlier), meant to withstand enemy bombing raids, hence the flat roof. It now also has metal sheeting covering most of the windows! Another downgrade came more recently when freight traffic from the adjacent quarry ceased.

There has been much made of the station with the longest name in Britain that lies on Anglesey, usually shortened to just Llanfair PG. Much less well known is its historical 1871-built signal box and gated level crossing, seen on a fine March evening in 2016 as No. 158818 arrives on a service to Holyhead. All being well, this box and all others west of Llandudno Junction on the North Wales Coast should survive until 2020.

Amid the barren countryside landscape on Anglesey lies the request stop station of Ty Croes, which still had a working (Grade II listed) box and gated level crossing in this March 2016 view. Note the staggered platforms and annex that was formerly the station building. The Down distant signal, which was still a semaphore at this time, was visible from the road around a mile east.

This picture of a Class 175 approaching Sutton Bridge Junction shows the variation in signalling to be found in the Shrewsbury area. The left-hand upper quadrant signal has a distant arm and below that, a smaller calling-on arm, which, if set 'off', allows a train to proceed at extreme caution into a section where another train may already be standing. The right-hand signal is GWR lower quadrant.

There are still four different working boxes at Shrewsbury and all have varying styles, mainly because the town's railways were shared between the GWR and LNWR (later LMS). The 1913-built Sutton Bridge Junction is GWR and controls movements towards either Aberystwyth or the Welsh Marches line via Craven Arms. Mercifully, it still retains its original five-pane window style despite conversion to uPVC types in recent years.

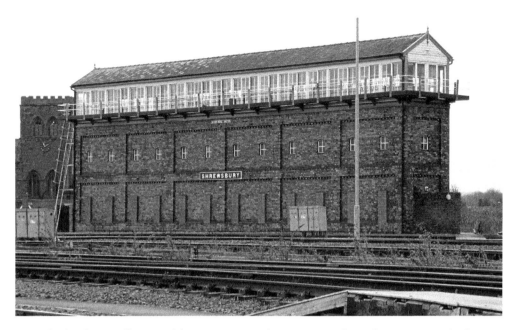

Now that's what I call a signal box! Severn Bridge Junction, Shrewsbury, is now the biggest working mechanical box in the world, holding 180 levers, and is double-manned by two signallers on a typical daytime shift, one controlling each end. It occupies the south end of Shrewsbury station at one end of a triangle towards Wolverhampton and the Cambrian/Welsh Marches lines. (Nick Jones, permission of Network Rail)

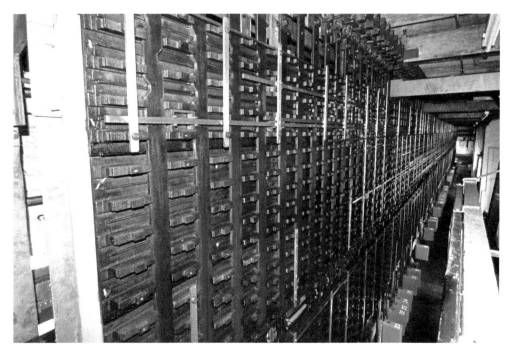

Within the bowels of Severn Bridge Junction box lies this massive lattice of signal interlocking bars, next to a narrow internal staircase that leads up to the third-floor operating room. It was constructed by the LNWR in 1903. (Nick Jones, permission of Network Rail)

Around half of Severn Bridge Junction's original 180 levers are still in use and this shot gives an impression of the sheer size. There are thirteen individual lines that are Absolute Block-worked: six to Abbey Foregate box, five to Crewe Junction box and two to Sutton Bridge Junction. Taken on 9 April 2016 during a visit by the Branch Line Society. (Nick Jones, permission of Network Rail)

An interesting relic inside Severn Bridge Junction box today is this LNWR train describer dating back to 1891. It is no longer in use but kept nicely polished. Signallers formerly used these to pass on information to the next box about the type and destination of an approaching train, for example, 'Engine for loop' or 'Empty coaches for siding' as shown here. They would rotate the needle by inserting a metal peg into the hole for the appropriate indication and it would transmit down via electrical pulses. (Nick Jones, permission of Network Rail)

The other Great Western box at Shrewsbury – Abbey Foregate – stands at another end of the triangle next to the station. There are three sets of double-track Absolute Block instruments inside, controlling the station bay platforms, the through lines and the side of the triangle seen diverging on the left that avoids the station and only sees one booked train (in one direction) per week at present. On the left background is Severn Bridge Junction box and on the right is the station approaches.

Severn Bridge Junction box viewed from Shrewsbury station. The upper quadrant semaphores seen here replaced the original lower quadrant GWR versions some time ago, but it was then discovered they could not be seen by train crews or platform staff due to the canopy! Signal posts with different heights were tried and there was also consideration given to cutting back the canopy before a solution was found by providing electronic 'OFF' indicators on the platform, which give advance warning of the signal positions.

Another hybrid system at Shrewsbury is this gantry at the north end of the station that carries colour lights plus a lower quadrant semaphore for the Down Platform line. The middle (Down Main) line was out of use by this time; note the lamp attached to the sleepers indicating it is closed off. On the left is Crewe Junction box, so called as this is where the route to Crewe (right) diverges from the line to Chester.

Crewe Junction box has 120 levers and is actually taller than the better known structure at Severn Bridge Junction. This shot gives the illusion that it sits at track level, when in fact it has a rear bricked base housing the locking frame stretching down to the bottom of the embankment on street level. No. 175006 coasts into the station on 30 March 2016.

Sprinter No. 150284 comes off the Chester line at Shrewsbury with a service for Birmingham New Street station on 30 March 2016.

CHAPTER 5

South West

Cornwall – a former stronghold of the GWR – retains a distinctive style of semaphore signalling largely unique to that part of the country. Our earlier study of the Shrewsbury area gave a taste of what to expect: lower quadrant semaphore signals, and lots of them. Their abundance means that the spirit of the GWR lives on in the twenty-first century and should do for a few years yet, until 2020 when mechanical signalling in the area is due to be eliminated and Didcot ROC will assume responsibility for most of south-west England.

While the other 'Big Four' companies – the Southern Railway (SR), London Midland & Scottish Railway (LMS) and London & North Eastern Railway (LNER) – phased out pre-grouping lower quadrant signals in favour of the upper quadrant, the GWR remained different. The upper quadrant was generally preferred because it was safer, as a broken signal wire would result in gravity forcing the signal arm into the 'danger' (horizontal) position. On lower quadrants, this could force it to drop and thus show 'clear'. The same could happen in the event of snow weighing down the arm. However, the Great Western found that the light spectacle (as provided on the right-hand side of each semaphore arm) could provide sufficient weight to balance out the weight of the arm dropping, so that even with a breakage, a lower quadrant signal would be forced to show 'danger'. As a result, the company stuck with its preferred design and they remained under the management of the BR Western Region, as the south-west geographical area became known. Thus, lower quadrant signals have stood the test of time in Cornwall and in other parts such as South Wales and Worcestershire.

The semaphores in Cornwall today are complemented by some historic boxes of different styles. Unlike a few of the GWR variants further north, they are very easy on the eye after refurbishment by Network Rail (and their predecessors Railtrack), with most replacement window panes following the original GWR pattern. Par and Lostwithiel are both platform-mounted while the rest are at track level.

At the centre of our focus is the Great Western main line from London Paddington to Penzance, which is mechanically signalled for most of the westernmost section into Cornwall. Semaphores also covered the Taunton–Plymouth section until it was re-signalled between 1985 and 1987, with Exeter PSB replacing all the manual boxes. Most of the route east of Westbury is now controlled by Didcot ROC and the Westbury–Exeter section should follow suit by 2026 if all goes to plan. This will see the closure of both Exeter and Westbury PSBs.

There is another power box further west at Plymouth, which controls most of the Great Western main line from Totnes to St Germans using TCB. This in turn is scheduled to give way to Didcot ROC in 2022. It was opened in 1960 when steam was still commonplace but its control sphere was very localised. In 1973, it took over control of the branch line to Gunnislake as well as the main line west to St Germans, resulting in the closure of boxes at Keyham, St Budeaux Road, Royal Albert Bridge and Saltash. Royal Albert Bridge box still stands today in railway office use. The same year, the famous Brunel-designed bridge itself was reduced to single-track (St Budeaux–Saltash). Plymouth PSB also took over in the east from the boxes at Mount Gould Junction, Laira Junction, Tavistock Junction, Hemerdon, Ivybridge and Brent. All of these box closures were a sign of things to come, but not until much later.

Liskeard, the junction for the branch to Looe, is where things start to get interesting. Westwards from here, there are seven boxes along the main line and semaphores galore. Absolute Block working mixes with Track Circuit Block in other sections, while the line is also single for two more very short stretches: for a mile between the viaducts at St Pinnock and East Largin, and a mile from Penzance station to Long Rock depot. The boxes are at Liskeard, Lostwithiel, Par, Truro, Roskear Junction, St Erth and Penzance. They survive along with those on the Newquay branch line at St Blazey and Goonbarrow Junction.

Just as Ayrshire is the land of the coalfield, Cornwall is indisputably china clay country. As with coal, the industry has declined in recent decades, but daily freights still operate centred around the St Blazey and Par area. One of several very scenic branch lines surviving in the region is the 4-mile freight-only route to Fowey Dock, which leaves the main line at Lostwithiel. It is a 'lock in': One Train Working using a staff, distributed by the signaller at Lostwithiel. The same method is used for the Burngullow Junction–Parkandillack branch.

The Par–Newquay branch gives access to St Blazey yard and locomotive depot, which lies just outside Par. It is double-track as far as St Blazey, with single-line Key Token working from there to the crossing loop at Goonbarrow Junction. From there to Newquay, it is One Train Working with a staff.

The branch to Looe and Moorswater is perhaps the most spectacular of all, as leaving Liskeard it dives down a steep gradient and burrows under the main line, turning about 360 degrees in the process. No Signalman Key Token working applies from Liskeard to Coombe Junction, and Coombe Junction to Moorswater cement terminal for freights. Passenger services need to reverse at Coombe Junction and a one-train staff gives access for the section to Looe. Freights to Moorswater are planned to restart in 2016 after a three-year absence.

One Train Working with staffs is the norm for the rest of the Cornish branches: to Gunnislake, St Ives and Falmouth, apart from Truro–Penryn on the Falmouth route, which is single-line TCB. On the St Ives branch, a DMU shuttles between there and St Erth throughout the day and the driver will have the staff in his or her possession the entire time as they have sole occupation of that section. Though there are one or two services early and late in the day that run straight through to or from Penzance, in which case the staff must be collected/surrendered when entering/exiting the branch. St Erth box is a GWR structure dating back to 1899, while Penzance's is from 1938 and only controls colour lights, the semaphores at the terminus being removed in 1981. Penzance is the southern-most station in Britain and most westerly in England (Arisaig is the most westerly in Britain).

Despite the short single-line sections, the Great Western main line remains busy, with HSTs running on average every two hours between Plymouth and Penzance, alongside

DMUs on various local services. A positive step during the last two summers has been the use of loco-hauled stock on Saturdays, when the Class 57 and seated coaches of the Night Riviera sleeper have been deployed during the day. Another recent development was operator First Great Western changing its name to Great Western Railway, as a homage to the original GWR, re-adopting the traditional dark green livery and 'shirt button' logo of the past.

While their present-day territory extends into Devon and much further east towards London, there is little of interest in terms of signalling in this direction. One exception is Crediton, where a box controls movements of trains either towards Barnstaple or diverging west to Okehampton and the Dartmoor heritage line. No Signaller Token Remote working is used on the Tarka line to Barnstaple. Crediton is expected to survive in use until 2026, when Exeter PSB shuts. Also worthy of mention to the south is Yeovil Pen Mill, the ex-GWR station serving the town of Yeovil alongside the SR's Yeovil Junction. The 1937 Great Western box (sixty-five levers) is due to be closed, with its semaphores swept away, before 2016 is out. It will join the many locations from the ex-Southern network now controlled by Basingstoke ROC.

Even more imminent is the demolition of the two GWR boxes at Banbury, on the Chiltern main line to Birmingham. It was the last station in the region to be mechanically controlled by a box at either end and as we speak, major work is underway to alter the track layout and signalling. This has brought about the demise of the North and South boxes, which controlled a varied mix of upper and lower quadrant semaphores as well as colour lights. Both remained in superb condition, and there was a local campaign to try to save the larger North cabin for use as an education centre, but this ultimately proved unsuccessful. They will now join the many other famous boxes in the history books.

BR-built Power Signal Boxes (PSBs) are also being phased out by ROCs. With simplified, electrically operated control panels replacing levers and with a wider control sphere, using colour light signals, they were seen as state-of-the-art when first introduced in the 1960s, yet they never managed to fully replace older, mechanical boxes. Exeter PSB, pictured here, overlooking St Davids station, was built in 1985 and could be closed by 2026, with its jurisdiction transferred to Didcot ROC.

Plymouth PSB was one of BR's earliest power boxes, commissioned back in 1960, and today controls the Great Western main line west almost as far as Liskeard (including the Gunnislake branch) and east to Totnes. It should close in 2022, when Didcot ROC assumes responsibility. A single-car Class 153 unit passes the box on its way out of Plymouth station on the evening of 23 May 2016.

Heading towards Penzance on the Great Western main line, GWR lower quadrant semaphores start appearing thick and fast after St Germans. A real rarity is this wooden-armed signal at Liskeard, seen opposite the box on 23 May 2016 as an HST departs for London Paddington. It is carried on a 'gallows'-style bracket and has an unusual centre-pivoted arm, built this way for visibility reasons.

Lostwithiel box (built in 1893 by the GWR) was recently Grade II listed, so the building should have a secure future once all manual signalling west of Plymouth is replaced in 2019. On 23 May 2016, No. 66027 accelerates over the level crossing with the 13.50 Fowey Dock (Carne Point)–Goonbarrow Junction china clay hoppers, having run round its train in the Up goods loop.

A four-car First Great Western Class 150 formation arrives at Lostwithiel with a service to Penzance, passing the mechanically signalled goods loops. It can be seen that the signal for the Down Main line has a sighting board. The railway formerly served a milk factory at this spot.

The 15.59 Penzance–Paddington HST, led by power car No. 43131, enters Lostwithiel on 23 May 2016, passing signal LL57 (LL is the abbreviation for Lostwithiel). It gives access to the sidings on the left that were used until recently for shunting the Fowey china clay trains.

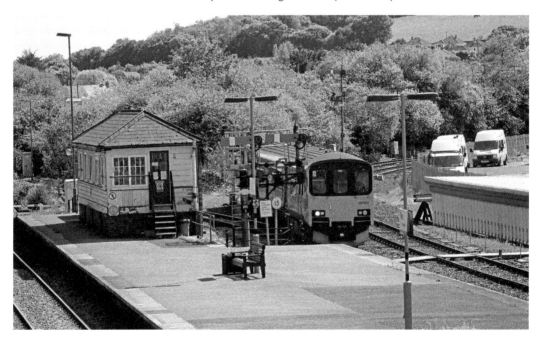

Par is the junction for Newquay via Goonbarrow Junction china clay terminal and St Blazey yard. On 23 May 2016, No. 150123 arrives with the 15.01 service from Newquay, coming off the branch which is guarded by a combined stop and distant signal seen in the background. Like many others left on the network, the distant is fixed at caution.

Middleway level crossing on the Newquay branch line. The single track into Par becomes double at this point, with the semaphore controlled by St Blazey box. This rural scene in fact lies just outside St Blazey yard and traction depot.

Roskear Junction, seen captured from a passing train, is probably Cornwall's least glamorous signal box, only controlling colour lights that are switch-operated instead of using a lever frame. It formerly gave access to a short branch serving a nearby factory and lies just east of Camborne station. One of the signaller's duties is to operate two nearby level crossings.

A First Great Western-liveried HST (power cars Nos 43139 and 43037) arrives at St Erth, the final stop before Penzance, with the 07.06 Paddington–Penzance on 24 May 2016. The St Ives branch can be seen diverging on the left. The signal furthest left is for branch trains leaving the bay platform, which is at a lower level than the main line platforms seen here.

The same HST arrives back into St Erth in the opposite direction forty minutes later with the 13.03 Penzance–Paddington. There is a starting signal at both platforms, as a couple of services from St Ives each day run through to Penzance instead of terminating here and have to use the Up platform, before using the crossover onto the Down line. The station is in excellent condition, apart from the weeds!

The GWR box at Penzance (seventy-five levers, built 1938) controls movements in and out of the terminus, though colour light signals have replaced semaphores. This view shows it from the platform ends. The line is single for about a mile east of here out to Long Rock depot, where the HSTs and overnight sleeper train from London are serviced.

Penzance box must have one of the best views of any in the UK, as this scene shows, looking out to the island of St Michael's Mount. Penzance is both the southern-most station in Britain and western-most in England.

CHAPTER 6

Anglia and South East

Mechanical signalling still dominates across much of the former BR Eastern Region, from East Anglia into Lincolnshire and along the borders of London Midland territory towards Nottingham. Norfolk is a particular highlight, despite the closure of all boxes along the Norwich–Ely line in 2012. East of Norwich, along the Wherry lines to Great Yarmouth and Lowestoft, the boxes and semaphore signals are still holding on, and the latest plan is to keep them in place until 2018, when the latest ETCS in-cab signalling will replace them. The change will be remarkable, as the signalling will essentially be skipping a few generations, without going through the usual change to colour lights.

The flat terrain of Norfolk and the Fens means that level crossings are dotted throughout and some on the Wherry lines are still manually worked gates. Two on the Brundall–Yarmouth via Acle line, situated in the Lingwood area, are manned with small lever frames but no signal box as such, similar to those examined earlier in Cumbria and Yorkshire. A few working distant semaphores are also still extant on the lines and there are swing bridges over rivers at Reedham and Somerleyton. At both these locations, there is a signal box to open and close the bridges, both Great Eastern Railway (GER) structures dating back to 1904. Due to their special functions, both boxes should survive the upcoming re-signalling programme and are likely to stay for a while to come.

The boxes that will close are Brundall, Acle, Yarmouth Vauxhall, Cantley, Reedham Junction, Oulton Broad North and Lowestoft. All are GER designs with Absolute Block working between all those on double-track sections. The two exceptions are the stretches Brundall–Yarmouth (via Acle) and Yarmouth–Reedham Junction, which are single-line and use the Tokenless Block method seen in Scotland. Acle has a crossing loop, while at Brundall station there is a hut used by a crossing keeper, separate from the signal box. The more modern BR-built panel box at Crown Point depot, Norwich, is scheduled to close in 2017. This is part of a separate scheme, as it controls part of the electrified line to Ipswich.

The 1987-built Trowse swing bridge box in Norwich, also on this route, should survive much longer than most of the others in the region. It won't outlive them though, as all the GER boxes are over 110 years old! As with the examples at Reedham and Somerleyton, Trowse is set to remain as no immediate decisions have been made about the future of the bridges. It operates the only electrified swing bridge in the UK, which uses an overhead conductor rail instead of wires. The bridge has been known to fail from time to time though and this can cut off Norwich to all services from the south. The fact it is a single-track structure is also a restriction.

Along with Crown Point, the boxes at Colchester (PSB), Parkeston (PSB) and Clacton are to shut in 2017, as is the GER gate box at Stowmarket on the electrified Norwich–Ipswich line. Further west, those on the Cambridge–Ipswich route at Bury St Edmunds Yard, Chippenham Junction and Dullingham will join them, along with Cambridge PSB. This clean sweep is part of the enlargement of Romford ROC, which will gradually assume control of East Anglia.

Further north, across the Fens into Cambridgeshire, it will be all change from 2020 to 2021. Boxes on the Ely–Peterborough stretch will close: those at Manea, Stonea, March South Junction, March East Junction, Three Horse Shoes, Whittlesea and Kings Dyke. The electrified line to King's Lynn will go the same way, with Littleport, Downham Market, Magdalen Road and King's Lynn all shutting. Ely itself was a great place to watch trains in the past with multiple joining routes and boxes, plus superb arrays of semaphores. These were lost in 1992 when the line to King's Lynn was electrified and Cambridge PSB took over.

Network Rail's re-signalling is certainly accelerating in the next couple of years, with the Nottingham–Lincoln line about to lose its boxes in late 2016, and Leicester–Peterborough set to follow suit the year after. Grantham–Skegness will gradually go the same way between 2019 and 2021. These boxes are a mixture of classic Midland & Great Northern Railway (GNR) designs. Plans are always subject to change of course, but on paper at least, it looks like this will be a watershed decade and the former Eastern Region will be virtually semaphore-free once we move into the 2020s.

The south-east, by contrast, is largely electrified with third-rail DC power and areas of manual signalling are few and far between. London in particular has moved on. The 4-mile Dudding Hill loop line is an exception; it is ex-LMS and not electrified. A freight-only byway, it holds a tiny pocket of semaphores within the city controlled by boxes at Dudding Hill Junction, Neasden Junction and Acton Canal Wharf. Greenford East box and its GWR lower quadrant signals also give some respite from the continual colour lights.

The South Coast termini of Bognor Regis and Littlehampton also retain some fine semaphores, which is unusual for that part of the country. The 1886-built Littlehampton box is a London, Brighton & South Coast Railway (LBSCR) design and has a very short time left in use, while the plainer, 1938 SR structure at Bognor has a closure date of 2018 lined up. Nearby Lancing, Barnham and Chicester boxes should shut along with Littlehampton, with the area thereafter worked by Three Bridges ROC near Crawley. Further east, Hastings also retains semaphores and is likely to survive until at least 2020. The same goes for Canterbury West that only controls colour lights, but has a grand position on a gantry above the tracks.

The scenic Medway Valley line from Strood to Paddock Wood is a highlight of Kent. Originally built by the South Eastern Railway (SER), it was electrified first from Strood to Maidstone West in 1939 and then along the rest of the line in 1961. Semaphore signals were replaced with colour lights in 2005, but the boxes themselves are still in use with Absolute Block working between them. A few still have gated level crossings as well. The boxes in question – Cuxton, Aylesford, Maidstone West, East Farleigh and Wateringbury – are set to survive for a few more years at least. Maidstone has another station on the London Victoria–Ashford line named Maidstone East. The box there is set to close during 2016.

The only location in Kent where semaphores can still be seen is Deal station on the Dover–Margate route. The box there, along with others on the line at Sandwich and Minster, should remain in place until at least 2020.

Trowse Swing Bridge, Norwich: the only electrified swing bridge in the UK. The box alongside was added in 1987 and now controls not only the bridge over the River Wensum, but most of the Norwich–Sheringham line. It replaced an earlier GER structure. On 10 July 2016, the 1530 London Liverpool St–Norwich crosses over, led by a DVT.

At Brundall, a hut is retained (right) for the crossing keeper who opens and shuts the gates, while the signaller works in a separate box. The vintage footbridge allows passengers to cross between the staggered platforms when the gates are closed to road traffic. On 10 July 2016, Turbostar DMU No. 170202 pauses with the 14.58 Norwich–Lowestoft.

The same unit departs past Brundall box, heading straight on at the junction towards Reedham and Lowestoft. Diverging left behind the '170' is the direct line to Great Yarmouth via Acle. Brundall box was opened in 1883 by the GER. The present frame – a McKenzie & Holland design with thirty-five levers – arrived in 1927, originating in another box.

Left: The third and final remaining co-acting signal on the Network Rail map is in the Down direction at Cantley, on the Norwich–Lowestoft line. On 10 July 2016, a pair of Class 153s is captured heading past.

Below: Cantley station, another example of the country level crossing scene that is disappearing fast. The box has had a very thorough refurbishment by Network Rail, with all external surfaces now uniform white uPVC. Note the height of the Down Platform starting signal.

At Great Yarmouth, the semaphores have had digital route indicators added to show whether trains are proceeding to Norwich via Acle or the other route through Reedham. Yarmouth Vauxhall box, pictured, is of 1884 GER vintage. A closer view was not possible without your humble author being dive-bombed by the local herring gulls!

Acle box is one of the more unusual GER examples in Norfolk, especially now it has been modernised to give the signaller a more pleasant working environment (see the replacement windows). It retains the same Saxby & Farmer 'Rocker'-type frame installed upon opening in 1883, containing twenty levers. Acle is a passing place on the single line between Brundall and Yarmouth.

The fine GER box at Bury St Edmunds Yard has been Grade II listed ahead of its planned closure in 2017. On 9 July 2016, Abellio Greater Anglia's No. 170205 passes, alongside the lightly used sidings.

In the Southern region, three ROCs at Basingstoke, Gillingham and Three Bridges are to take over the few remaining mechanical signal boxes. The 1962 BR power box at Tonbridge will also close, during 2018. It is seen on 13 July 2016, with no less than six GBRf Class 73s visible alongside in the freight yard.

The picturesque Medway Valley line from Strood to Paddock Wood lost its semaphores in 2005, but there are still manual boxes (controlling colour lights) and gated crossings along this third-rail electric route. Class 466 Networker No. 466034 arrives at Wateringbury on 12 July 2016 with the 17.15 for Strood. The 1893 box is Grade II listed, as is the rest of the station, including the goods shed to the right.

East Farleigh box is a product of the SER dating back to 1892, now with a reduced frame of eleven levers. A modern addition to this rural station is LED train departure boards; one can be seen on the far platform.

With the fine Maidstone West box towering behind, No. 66094 heads a rake of empty box wagons from East Peckham Tip to Southall on 12 July 2016. Beside me on the platform was a Belgian railway photographer, on holiday from his day job driving freight trains between France and the port of Antwerp.

Maidstone East, a 1962 BR-built structure that holds one of the last few miniature lever frames in Britain. A Westinghouse 'L' frame, it was formerly in place at London Cannon Street station, and in addition to that there is an NX panel that controls the box's outer limits on the London Victoria–Ashford line. This shot was taken on 12 July 2016, not long before the box's scheduled closure.

CHAPTER 7

Heritage Signal Boxes

Working mechanical signalling with semaphores has been part and parcel of the UK heritage railway scene for decades, and a great number of boxes (and signals) have been saved for a new lease of life on preserved lines up and down the country. Not only does this require a lot of time and money for restoration, but also the resources to be able to move a building, either whole or dismantled in 'kit' form where possible.

There is also a commendable amount of disused boxes on the main line that are still standing, some derelict but many in great condition that have been adapted for other uses. With Network Rail's recent Operating Strategy being unveiled and hundreds being gradually decommissioned as we speak, there is a race against time to save as many of these magnificent Victorian buildings from the axe as possible.

Thankfully, almost 200 boxes across the country have been listed at the time of writing as they are quite rightly seen as icons of British history and architecture (most are on the main line but some are preserved). Thus they are protected from demolition. Those in England (administered by English Heritage, now rebranded Historic England) and Wales (by Cadw) are classified with a listing status of either Grade I, Grade II* or Grade II, with Grade I being the highest, according to their level of historical or architectural interest. In Scotland (administered by Historic Scotland), they are classified in descending order as either Grade A, B or C. The majority of signal boxes are Grade II or Grade B if they are Scottish. Five in Scotland are of the highest category, Grade A: Broughty Ferry, Stirling Middle, Stirling North, Pitlochry and the relocated preserved box at Bo'ness. Sat at Scotland's oldest station, Broughty Ferry was unusually attached to the timber footbridge and closed in 1995, before being temporarily dismantled, restored and relocated on the opposite platform.

The West Highland line from Glasgow to Fort William is a good example where redundant main line boxes have fared well. Most being of a design unique to that route in a style similar to the 'Swiss chalet' station buildings, there was always a desire to keep these types intact. All were officially closed in 1988 with the introduction of RETB signalling but the majority have found alternative use (only the conventional Glen Douglas was demolished). A particularly shrewd move was the refurbishment of those at Arrochar & Tarbet and Ardlui to convert them into waiting rooms. Being mounted on the platforms with windows all around, the tiny cabins are ideal for this purpose. Indeed, an additional waiting room was built at Arrochar in 2000 as almost an exact replica!

Other boxes on the West Highland line have invariably been used as stores following closure and have generally been kept in good condition. Rannoch has been nicely preserved and turned into a mini visitor centre, with the Saxby & Farmer seventeen-lever frame still intact. Tulloch is another one that retains its levers and holds a water supply used for the station hostel. The lever frames from Arrochar and Upper Tyndrum have gone to the Leadhills & Wanlockhead Railway and the Invergarry Station Preservation Society respectively.

Glenfinnan box, on the West Highland Mallaig Extension, has been beautifully preserved as part of the station museum there. It was designed and built by contractors the Railway Signal Co. for the West Highland Railway, in a completely different style to those south of Fort William, for the line's opening in 1901. The fifteen-lever frame (a Stevens design) is not only still in situ but also in partial working order. Volunteers provide regular signalling demonstrations for visitors, working the levers and using video monitors to show how the semaphores used to be pulled off. Glenfinnan, like Barrhill on the Stranraer line, originally had its block instruments located in the station building, with the levers in the box. Tablets would be swapped by hand and latterly the sections were to Arisaig in the west and Annat (near Fort William) in the east. Both instruments still sit in the same spot today, preserved as part of the museum in the old stationmaster's office, with working bell and gong. The Glasgow–Fort William and Mallaig lines were originally owned by the independent West Highland Railway but operated by the North British Railway, before the LNER took over in 1923.

Many boxes on heritage railways are originals that were in situ in the days of the working railway. Levisham on the North Yorkshire Moors Railway, for example, has been in the same spot since 1876 when the Pickering–Grosmont route was under the stewardship of the North Eastern Railway. But many are disused structures from other locations that have been re-erected, a practice that has saved numerous main line boxes. A great working example is that at Bo'ness station on the Bo'ness & Kinneil Railway, formerly of Garnqueen South Junction near Coatbridge. The A-listed cabin was built by the Caledonian Railway in 1899 and controls some wonderful lower quadrant semaphores, mostly rescued from Coupar Angus on the 'Caley' main line to Aberdeen. Also notable is Butterley box on the Midland Railway Centre's line, formerly of Ais Gill on the S&C route.

Crewe Heritage Centre is a fascinating place to visit, as there are three signal boxes of vastly different types restored to their original condition both inside and out. The main one, Crewe North Junction, remains in its rightful place beside the station overlooking the junction between the WCML and the line to Chester. The full Westinghouse 'L' miniature lever frame formerly controlled movements north to Crewe Coal Yard box, also built in 1939 by the LMS. It is interesting to note that the latter, pictured on page 21, is still in normal use for Network Rail. Also at the centre are the old LNWR Crewe 'A' box (originally located within the station) and GWR Exeter West, which was one of three mechanical boxes located at Exeter St Davids station until 1985 when they were replaced by the power box there (see page 71).

The 1948-built Nantwich box on the Crewe–Shrewsbury line has been moved and re-erected in Crewe also, serving a useful function as a training base for new rail staff with the engineering firm OSL. It faced demolition after all boxes on that route were decommissioned in 2013, with control passing to Cardiff ROC.

There has not always been a happy ending for disused boxes in recent years though, even with campaigns and strong local support. The plight of the two historic structures at Banbury is a prime example of this. The box at Dawlish station on the Great Western main line also springs to mind, having lain disused for years after closing in 1986. It was an elegant 1918-built GWR design with a sloping, narrow base that allowed it to fit on the platform and so was deemed to be of major historical and architectural importance. However, years of inactivity on an exposed sea wall did it no favours and the structure gradually fell into disrepair. Despite being listed by English Heritage, it was de-listed and demolished in 2013. Its condition had deteriorated to the point that any restoration project for possible alternative use was not considered worthwhile.

The picture is not all bad in Devon and Cornwall though. The GWR box at Totnes station is a large 1923-vintage structure that closed in 1987 but is Grade II listed and now in use as a café. Bodmin Parkway station box is also a café, located on the main line platform one next to where the preserved Bodmin & Wenford Railway branch diverges. It is run by staff from the heritage line and is Grade II as well.

Both McKenzie & Holland design boxes at Nairn on the Inverness–Aberdeen line closed in 2000 but are now Grade B listed. They are disused but have been well preserved with levers intact, and Network Rail are still required to keep the interiors in good order. On this day in June 2015, there was movement inside Nairn East box for once, as the door was open for members of the Branch Line Society on an organised day out. (Author, permission of Network Rail)

At the opposite end of the station is Nairn West, formerly the main box, with nineteen levers (East box has thirteen). This June 2015 interior view shows it to be in good condition. Someone at Network Rail still has the bicycle formerly used by the signalman to move between the two boxes! (Author, permission of Network Rail)

Glenfinnan box in the West Highlands, where regular signalling demonstrations are held with the aid of video monitors (see top right). The locking room is used as a cinema. Note also the station track diagrams. (Nick Jones)

The whole station at Stirling is Grade A listed, including the two remaining signal boxes, though 2013 saw most of the semaphores removed. On 16 September 2015, ultra-modern No. 68002 *Intrepid* passes the Middle box on 4A13, the afternoon Grangemouth–Aberdeen containers.

Ravenglass box on the Cumbrian Coast route is now closed but has been restored inside and out by volunteers from the narrow gauge Ravenglass & Eskdale Railway, based next to the main line station. Standing high on a cutting, this FR Cabin is 142 years old.

Still operational on the Cumbrian Coast, Arnside was recently Grade II listed along with a number of other boxes on the network, such as Garsdale, Skegness and Downham Market. Constructed in 1897, this stone-built gem is expected to stay in use until 2021.

Settle station box closed in 1984 but has been magnificently preserved by the Friends of the Settle–Carlisle Line. A MR type 2a design, it was relocated 150 yards north of its original trackside position. It now forms a signalling museum.

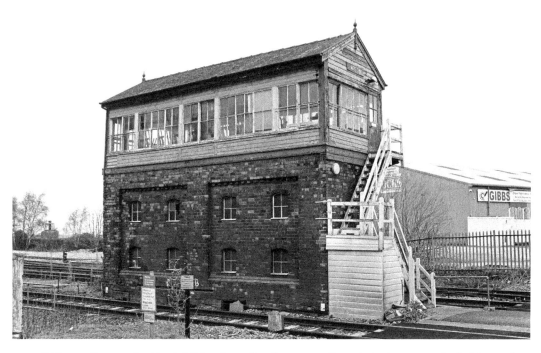

Still standing on the North Wales Coast line but normally switched out, 1902-built Mostyn box is Grade II listed. It is not in the best condition but its appearance is largely unchanged from LNWR days, without being spoilt by uPVC-lined windows.

The gate box at Damems on the preserved Keighley & Worth Valley Railway was relocated from Earby station on the closed Skipton–Colne line. The larger box that controls the nearby crossing loop came from Frizinghall, near Bradford. Damems is said to be the smallest full-size station in Britain.

Still in the same spot where it was built 140 years ago, the NER box at Levisham station on the North Yorkshire Moors Railway controls a level crossing and a well-used loop on the single line. Before preservation, it was a gate box only and not a block post. This remote spot is accessed via a very steep and twisty single-track road.

GWR-built Bodmin Parkway station box has been turned into a café. In this May 2016 view, it appears that work is in progress to add a new entrance porch and replace the outer timber frames.

There was a happy ending for Wroxham box on the Norwich–Cromer/Sheringham line, closed in 2000 but now restored by the Wroxham Signal Box Trust. It is a GER design from 1900. Built alongside it is the 15-inch gauge Bure Valley Railway, seen on 10 July 2016, with locomotive No. 7 *Spitfire* on the turntable.

Maidstone West is a unique design that is now Grade II listed. It is a product of Evans, O'Donnell & Co., built for the SER in 1899 and propped up on a narrow brick base. Most of its 115 levers are now disused.

Bibliography

Websites

www.foscl.org.uk
www.historic-scotland.gov.uk
www.historicengland.org.uk
www.networkrail.co.uk
www.railwaysarchive.co.uk
www.realtimetrains.co.uk
www.signalbox.org
www.s-r-s.org.uk

Reading List

Branch Line News
Hall, Stanley, *BR Signalling Handbook* (Shepperton: Ian Allan, 1992).
Kay, Peter, *Signalling Atlas and Signal Box Directory*, Third Edition (Wallasey: Signalling Record Society, 2010).
Network Rail, *Route Specifications 2014 London North Eastern & the East Midlands*.
RAIL magazine.
Railway Track Diagrams Nos 1–5 (Track Maps).
Smith, David L., *Legends of the Glasgow & South Western Railway in LMS Days* (Vermont: David & Charles, 1980).
Vanns, Michael A., *Signalboxes*, Second Edition (Hersham: Ian Allan, 2013).